HORN

Audio arrangements by Peter Deneff

To access audio, visit:
www.halleonard.com/mylibrary

"Enter Code"
1499-8758-8688-3177

ISBN 978-1-5400-9212-0

HAL•LEONARD®

For all works contained herein:
Unauthorized copying, arranging, adapting, recording, Internet posting, public performance,
or other distribution of the music in this publication is an infringement of copyright.
Infringers are liable under the law.

Visit Hal Leonard Online at
www.halleonard.com

Contact us:
Hal Leonard
7777 West Bluemound Road
Milwaukee, WI 53213
Email: info@halleonard.com

In Europe, contact:
Hal Leonard Europe Limited
42 Wigmore Street
Marylebone, London, W1U 2RN
Email: info@halleonardeurope.com

In Australia, contact:
Hal Leonard Australia Pty. Ltd.
4 Lentara Court
Cheltenham, Victoria, 3192 Australia
Email: info@halleonard.com.au

CONTENTS

BAD GUY

Horn

Words and Music by BILLIE EILISH O'CONNELL
and FINNEAS O'CONNELL

Copyright © 2019 UNIVERSAL MUSIC CORP., DRUP and LAST FRONTIER
All Rights for DRUP Administered by UNIVERSAL MUSIC CORP.
All Rights for LAST FRONTIER Administered Worldwide by KOBALT SONGS MUSIC PUBLISHING
All Rights Reserved   Used by Permission

I LOVE YOU

Horn

Words and Music by BILLIE EILISH O'CONNELL
and FINNEAS O'CONNELL

Copyright © 2019 UNIVERSAL MUSIC CORP., DRUP and LAST FRONTIER
All Rights for DRUP Administered by UNIVERSAL MUSIC CORP.
All Rights for LAST FRONTIER Administered Worldwide by KOBALT SONGS MUSIC PUBLISHING
All Rights Reserved   Used by Permission

EVERYTHING I WANTED

Horn

Words and Music by BILLIE EILISH O'CONNELL
and FINNEAS O'CONNELL

Copyright © 2019 UNIVERSAL MUSIC CORP., DRUP and LAST FRONTIER
All Rights for DRUP Administered by UNIVERSAL MUSIC CORP.
All Rights for LAST FRONTIER Administered Worldwide by KOBALT SONGS MUSIC PUBLISHING
All Rights Reserved   Used by Permission

Idontwannabeyouanymore

Horn

Words and Music by BILLIE EILISH O'CONNELL
and FINNEAS O'CONNELL

Copyright © 2018 UNIVERSAL MUSIC CORP., DRUP and LAST FRONTIER
All Rights for DRUP Administered by UNIVERSAL MUSIC CORP.
All Rights for LAST FRONTIER Administered Worldwide by KOBALT SONGS MUSIC PUBLISHING
All Rights Reserved   Used by Permission

LOVELY

Horn

Words and Music by BILLIE EILISH O'CONNELL,
FINNEAS O'CONNELL and KHALID ROBINSON

Copyright © 2018 UNIVERSAL MUSIC CORP., DRUP, LAST FRONTIER and SONY/ATV MUSIC PUBLISHING LLC
All Rights for DRUP Administered by UNIVERSAL MUSIC CORP.
All Rights for LAST FRONTIER Administered Worldwide by KOBALT SONGS MUSIC PUBLISING
All Rights for SONY/ATV MUSIC PUBLISHING LLC Administered by SONY/ATV MUSIC PUBLISHING LLC, 424 Church Street, Suite 1200, Nashville, TN 37219
All Rights Reserved   Used by Permission

NO TIME TO DIE

Horn

Words and Music by BILLIE EILISH O'CONNELL
and FINNEAS O'CONNELL

Copyright © 2020 UNIVERSAL MUSIC CORP., DRUP, U/A MUSIC, INC. and LAST FRONTIER
All Rights for DRUP and U/A MUSIC, INC. Administered by UNIVERSAL MUSIC CORP.
All Rights for LAST FRONTIER Administered Worldwide by KOBALT SONGS MUSIC PUBLISHING
All Rights Reserved   Used by Permission

OCEAN EYES

Horn

Words and Music by
FINNEAS O'CONNELL

Copyright © 2016 Last Frontier
All Rights Administered Worldwide by Kobalt Songs Music Publishing
All Rights Reserved   Used by Permission

YOU SHOULD SEE ME IN A CROWN

Horn

Words and Music by BILLIE EILISH O'CONNELL
and FINNEAS O'CONNELL

Copyright © 2018 UNIVERSAL MUSIC CORP., DRUP and LAST FRONTIER
All Rights for DRUP Administered by UNIVERSAL MUSIC CORP.
All Rights for LAST FRONTIER Administered Worldwide by KOBALT SONGS MUSIC PUBLISHING
All Rights Reserved   Used by Permission

WHEN THE PARTY'S OVER

HORN

Words and Music by
FINNEAS O'CONNELL

Copyright © 2018 Last Frontier
All Rights Administered Worldwide by Kobalt Songs Music Publishing
All Rights Reserved   Used by Permission